The lost link

Uncovering the Pattern That Connects Myth, Science and Algorithms.

Tanvi Nagare

Copyright

Some passages reflect personal perspectives and interpretations.

Readers are encouraged to engage with the ideas in their own way.

ISBN : 978-93-5602-439-7

Printed in india

To dad,

Thankyou for the real stories and
the conversations that shaped me.
If it weren't for that day, this
book wouldn't exist

Contents

Introduction

Chapter 1 : The lost link between science and faith

Chapter 2 : The Split That Never Existed

Chapter 3 : The First Pattern

Chapter 4 : The Story Behind Every Story

Chapter 5 : When Humans Started Looking Up

Chapter 6 : The Mirror of Consciousness

Chapter 7 : The Myth of Separation

Chapter 8 : The Architects of Attention

Chapter 9 : One Story, Many Languages

Chapter 10 : The Pattern We Are Creating

Conclusion

Introduction

I didn't plan to write a book.
I just followed a trail of questions that refused to leave me alone.

It started when I noticed something strange:
the deeper I looked into different religions — and even science —
the more they began to echo each other.
Not in language, but in structure.
Not in rituals, but in patterns.

At first, it was just a private curiosity.
A few notes.
A theory.
A thought I assumed would fade.

Instead, it grew.
And the more I tried to ignore it, the louder it became.

So I wrote.

Not to prove anything.
Not to preach.
But to understand.

You're about to walk through the thoughts that lived in my head long before they made it onto paper.

Nothing here is absolute; it's simply my attempt to trace the hidden lines that connect belief, story, logic, and the human need for meaning.

If you're holding this book, then you're curious too.
That's where my journey began.

Let's explore the patterns together.

Chapter 1 : The lost link between science and faith

At the end of the day, every holy book points toward the same thing.

Be kind. Show mercy. Help one another.

Whether it is the Bhagavad Gita, the Quran, the Bible, or the Guru Granth Sahib, the core message doesn't change.

Each asks us to live with compassion, not chaos.

Somewhere along the way, we let that slip.

We started fighting over which text was "right" and ignored the fact that they all point toward the same truth.

Kindness. Balance. Creation. Light.

No, I haven't read every scripture cover to cover.

But when you zoom out far enough, the patterns blur into one idea that's almost impossible to miss.

Maybe the argument was never between faiths.

Maybe it was between faith and science—two perspectives we convinced ourselves cannot coexist.

Somewhere, we stopped seeing them as two versions of the same story.

Holy places, regardless of religion, exist for the same reason.

To pray.

To remember.

To pause in lives that never slow down.

When we stand in a temple or a mosque, a church or a gurudwara, we're doing the same thing.

We reach toward something greater than ourselves, even if we call it by different names.

That feeling—quiet, steady, ancient—is older than every scripture ever written.

It links us to the people before us, the ones who looked up at the same sky and wondered how it all began.

Before the labels. Before the borders. Before the divisions.

There was only wonder.

So what if science and faith were never enemies at all?

What if they're just two languages describing the same truth—one through logic and one through symbols?

We see rituals in religion.

We see equations in science.

But maybe both are trying to explain the same miracle: how something rose from nothing, how order emerged from chaos, and how life climbed toward consciousness.

Maybe the link between faith and science was never lost.

Maybe we just stopped listening to both at the same time.

If two systems look different but lead to the same truth, then something deeper is at work.

And if the link was never truly broken, then the next question becomes impossible to ignore:

Where did both begin telling the same story long before we had the words to realise it?

Chapter 2 : The Split That Never Existed

What if evolution wasn't discovered, but remembered?

What if the oldest myths were not fiction, but memory preserved in symbols?

Ancient Hindu texts seem to describe the same stages of evolution that modern science uncovered recently.

Look at the beginning of the Dashavatara.

Matsya, the fish, represents the first movement of life through water.

Then Kurma, the turtle, rising onto land.

Then Varaha, the boar, standing firmly on earth.

Each avatar echoes a shift in life's journey—from water to land to increasing complexity.

Maybe these stories were never meant to be literal.

Maybe they were a symbolic record of evolution, written long before science had words for cells, fossils, or genetics.

A way of capturing the rhythm of life without microscopes or measurements.

And these ideas don't stand alone.

Many cultures carry memories of great floods.

Noah in Christianity.

Nuh in Islam.

Manu in Hindu tradition.

Stories of cleansing, renewal, and beginnings.

Science calls these moments mass extinctions and evolutionary resets.

Different words, same truth.

Maybe the creator didn't control every event directly.

Maybe the creator initiated a process—a sequence designed to unfold on its own.

Maybe evolution isn't a contradiction to faith, but faith expressed through nature's laws.

What if creation wasn't a single act, but an ongoing movement?

A universe set in motion, guided by principles so precise that life could rise from water, crawl onto land, and eventually look back and question its own origin.

Perhaps the divine didn't write evolution.

Perhaps the divine wrote the conditions that made evolution possible.

But if ancient stories truly carried echoes of evolution, then another possibility opens up :

what if symbols weren't just metaphors, but the way early humans translated transformation itself?

To see that, we need to look at how myth and biology mirror each other far more closely than we were ever taught.

Chapter 3 : The First Pattern

The ancients didn't have microscopes, DNA models, or scientific terminology.

What they had were symbols.

Stories.

Patterns woven into myths that carried truths too large to express directly.

When they spoke of gods transforming—from fish to man, from instinct to intellect—maybe they weren't imagining divine beings changing shape.

Maybe they were describing life itself transforming.

Maybe they were recording evolution in the only language they had.

They didn't call it "natural selection."

But they watched the world closely.

They saw life rising from water, adapting to land, learning to survive, learning to think.

And they turned those observations into symbolic narratives that survived thousands of years.

Science explains this journey with fossils, mutations, and genetic drift.

Faith explains it with stories of creation, avatars, and divine progression.

But beneath the different languages, both point to the same movement:

life taking form, rising in complexity, reaching toward consciousness.

Maybe evolution isn't evidence against the divine.

Maybe it's evidence of how the divine works.

What if every stage of evolution wasn't random at all, but a reflection of a deeper order?

What if each symbolic avatar represented not just physical change, but moral evolution too?

A lesson for humanity hidden within the growth of life itself.

Because evolution is not only about bodies changing.

It is about awareness expanding.

It is about learning compassion over survival, conscience over instinct.

Maybe the rise of consciousness wasn't an accident.

Maybe it was the point all along.

If myth and evolution overlap so precisely, then maybe the connection isn't limited to one culture.

Maybe every religion, in its own language, was trying to map the same cycle of beginning, becoming, and awareness.

To understand that, we have to look across traditions, not just within one.

Chapter 4 : The Story Behind Every Story

Across religions, the stories differ in detail, language, and symbolism.

But when you strip away the surface, a shared pattern begins to appear.

A movement from creation, to transformation, to consciousness.

Christianity speaks of a universe created from nothing, unfolding in stages.

Not instantly, but step by step, structured and intentional.

Science describes a similar process : the expansion of the universe, the slow rise of life, evolution across time.

Different descriptions, same sequence.

Order emerging from emptiness.

Hinduism describes creation as a cycle, an endless rhythm of expansion and contraction.

Vishnu's breath becomes universes, Brahma shapes diversity, and the avatars echo evolution itself.

Not a single beginning, but a repeating transformation, much like how cosmology describes the universe expanding, cooling, collapsing, and beginning again.

Islam tells of the heavens and earth once being joined, then separated.

It speaks of all life emerging from water.

Science echoes this : a singular cosmic origin, and the first life beginning in the oceans.

Again, different vocabulary, same underlying structure.

When you align these narratives, the pattern becomes sharp and unmistakable:

Creation → Transformation → Consciousness

A universe emerging from nothing.

Life arising from water.

Complexity increasing.

Awareness awakening.

The symbols change, the language shifts, but the story remains the same.

Everything began as a spark, unfolded in stages, and moved towards beings capable of thought, emotion, and morality.

When you look past the rituals, past the literal interpretations, you find that every faith and every scientific theory is trying to describe the same journey.

From nothing to something.

From particles to people.

From existence to awareness.

And that journey is still going on.

And once these patterns line up across faiths and scientific theories, a question rises.

What does all of this mean for us?

Because creation didn't end in ancient time; it's still unfolding, and humanity is now part of its next step.

Chapter 5 : When Humans Started Looking Up

From the first cell to the first thought, everything has been moving in one direction—

not away from the divine, but toward understanding it.

The link between science and faith was never broken.

We just stopped paying attention.

Science asks *how* life began.

Faith asks *why*.

Science studies creation from the outside.

Faith experiences it from within.

But both describe the same movement :

Energy shaping itself into structure, structure shifting into life, life unfolding into awareness.

If evolution is the universe's method, then it isn't finished.

It didn't stop with bodies or instincts.

It continues through us—through every act of empathy, every idea that expands consciousness, every time a human refuses ignorance and chooses clarity.

The next step in evolution isn't physical.

It's moral.

Maybe the "final avatar" isn't a warrior descending from the sky.

Maybe the final avatar is awareness itself—

a generation learning to cut through noise, greed, illusion, choosing wisdom over chaos.

Maybe the "end" isn't destruction.

Maybe it's awakening.

Faith shaped our hearts.

Science shaped our minds.

The future depends on both learning to work together, not as rivals, but as two tools aimed at the same question :

Where did we come from, where are we going?

Creation didn't end billions of years ago.

It didn't end in scripture either.

It's still unfolding—right now—in every conscious decision we make.

This isn't the last chapter of creation.

It's simply the first one we're finally aware of.

Chapter 6 : The Mirror of Consciousness

If the evolution of the universe brought us to awareness, then the real question is:

What do we do with that awareness?

We evolve every time we pay attention to something.

A thought becomes a pattern.

A pattern becomes identity.

Identity becomes behaviour.

And behaviour becomes the next version of us.

Evolution didn't end with Homo sapiens.

It simply shifted location.

From the body to the mind.

Today, our growth is psychological, intellectual, and digital.

Every idea we let in reshapes us

Every story, every influence, every algorithm we interact with doesn’t just touch us.

They rewire us.

The avatars of today are not physical forms.

They are mental states.

Ancient evolution changed bodies.

Modern evolution changes consciousness.

Global culture, the internet, AI, constant information—these aren't distractions from evolution.

They're the environment of a new kind of hyper-evolution we barely understand.

For thousands of years, evolution was unconscious.

Now, for the first time, humans can choose what they evolve into.

And once we recognise this, we can't pretend we're passive product of our surroundings.

The more clearly we see it, the more self-aware we become.

Maybe the next stage of evolution won't give us wings or telepathy.

Maybe it demands something tougher :

psychological flexibility, emotional precision, attention mastery, the courage to outgrow inherited beliefs, the intelligence to use technology without becoming dependent on it.

Refusing to evolve is not neutrality.

It is decay.

And decay eventually leads to extinction.

Harsh, yes.

But true.

Creation did not end.

Awareness started.

And now, you, I, and everyone alive today are shaping the next step—not accidentally, but consciously.

Which leaves us with a question we can't dodge :

If we are evolving with awareness, what exactly are we evolving toward?

The moment consciousness enters evolution, the process stops being random.

It becomes intentional.

Shaped by our choices, our environments, and the systems we build.

The future isn't something that "arrives" anymore.

It's something we're constructing—often without realising it.

Chapter 7 : The Myth of Separation

Nothing ever happens suddenly.

The ideas we think we "discover" are usually the ones that have been forming beneath the surface for years.

We just notice then the moment they break through.

We pretend evolution is unpredictable, but it follows patterns that are almost mechanical.

The sequence repeats itself :

thoughts → actions → outcomes → consequences

And every consequence becomes the starting point for the next stage of evolution.

A repeated thought becomes a belief.

A belief alters a decision.

A decision shifts a path.

And one small shift eventually reshapes the future.

That is how evolution actually happens :

Slowly, Silently, Relentlessly.

Most people move through this unconsciously.

A few make their choices consciously.

And the difference between the two trajectories becomes enormous over time.

Whether we like it or not, we are the writers of the next chapter of evolution.

Repeating the same patterns leads to decay.

Studying the patterns consciously creates change.

Evolution is predictable because patterns are predictable.

If we want to know our future, we have to study the patterns we're reinforcing today.

And If our patterns shape our evolution, then the next question becomes unavoidable:

who is shaping our patterns?

Because in the modern world, our attention isn't just influenced — it's engineered.

And understanding that is the key to understanding the next phase of evolution.

Chapter 8 : The Architects of Attention

If evolution today is shaped by patterns, then we have to understand the forces designing those patterns.

Religion, science, culture, media, and modern algorithms all claim to guide us, but in reality they guide our attention.

And whatever controls attention controls evolution.

Ancient religions shaped human behaviour through stories, symbols, laws, rituals, promises, and fear.

They determined what people should focus on, what they should avoid, what they should worship, and what they should never question.

Early science shaped behaviour differently.

It redirected human attention toward discovery, tools, technology, and observation.

What people once called divine became measurable.

What was once myth turned into method.

Today, algorithms shape behaviour by controlling what we notice and what we ignore.

They decide what rises, what disappears, what trends, and what dies without ever being seen.

Different systems, same function.

Religious, scientific, and digital structures all influence human evolution by guiding how we think and where our attention goes.

Every major shift in human consciousness has always been triggered by attention.

What a civilisation worships, studies, fears, celebrates, or consumes.

And whenever attention gets pulled too far in one direction, the balance breaks.

That imbalance eventually creates conflict, collapse, or a transformation that becomes the next avatar of human behaviour.

None of this is sudden.

Every era has had its own attention trap.

We only recognise it once we begin questioning the system shaping us.

Attention has always been engineered.

It has always been the hidden force behind every evolutionary leap.

And it still is.

Once we see how these systems direct our attention, something becomes impossible to ignore :

religion, science, and even technology are not separate worlds.

They are different ways of describing the same truth.

And when you place them side by side, the divisions we were taught to believe in start to dissolve, revealing one story told in different languages.

Chapter 9 : One Story, Many Languages

People fight over religion, science, and belief systems because they only look at the surface.

But the moment you go deeper, you realise they're all trying to answer the same questions:

how the world began, how it works, and why it changes.

Creation myths talk about order rising from chaos.

Gods represent forces of nature or parts of human psychology.

Judgement, karma, heaven and hell are just moral consequences written as stories.

Cycles of birth and destruction mirror entropy, renewal, expansion, and collapse.

Religion explains the universe through symbols.

Science uses formulas to describe the same patterns.

The Big Bang is a creation moment.

Evolution is continuous transformation.

Entropy is decay and destruction.

Quantum mechanics describes invisible forces shaping reality.

Cosmology explains cycles of expansion, collapse, and rebirth.

The modern digital world uses yet another language.

Networks, algorithms, and information systems describe the same patterns but in data form.

Zoom out and it becomes obvious:

Religion is symbolic explanation.

Science is physical explanation.

The digital world is informational explanation.

Different languages.

One underlying story.

Patterns create reality.

Reality evolves.

Consciousness adapts.

And if evolution is shaped by patterns, then something or someone is shaping the patterns.

Earlier, we asked whether religions and science point to the same truth.

This chapter shows they always have.

Most conflicts exist because people mistake different translations of the same idea for different truths.

And once this becomes visible, the real question becomes unavoidable:

What story are we creating for the next generation?

Because in the digital age, we are not just interpreting the universe.

We are rewriting it.

Chapter 10 : The Pattern We Are Creating

From the first myth to the latest equation, humanity has only been asking one question in a thousand different languages.

And we've always received the same answer.

Just expressed differently.

That is what eventually created conflicts.

This whole book was basically asking one thing:

were these thousand "languages" ever separate,

or were they always translations of the same truth?

Religion is a symbolic pattern language

Creation → order from chaos

Gods → forces of nature or psychology

Karma and judgment → moral cause and effect

Cycles → entropy and renewal

Science is a physical pattern language

Big Bang, evolution, entropy, quantum mechanics, cosmology

The digital world is an informational pattern language

Algorithms, networks, data cycles, attention systems

Different languages.

Same structure underneath.

That is why arguments about "religion vs religion vs science" are shallow.

Not because people lack intelligence,

but because they focus only on the surface.

These systems aren't contradicting each other.

They're translating the same story in different formats.

Conflicts happen only because translations get mistaken for separate truths.

And as we've seen throughout these chapters,

evolution is shaped by patterns—

genetic, cosmic, cultural, and informational.

If patterns shape reality,

then whoever builds the patterns shapes reality.

Religion gave us mythic patterns.

Science gave us empirical patterns.

Digital systems now create algorithmic patterns.

We have moved from discovering patterns

to designing them.

The modern world doesn't merely interpret the universe.

We build digital ecosystems.

We craft narratives.

We write code.

We create new forms of intelligence.

If humans now generate patterns

that guide how billions think, behave, and evolve,

then whatever we create next becomes

the next religion,

the next science

the next story of the universe.

So the final question becomes:

What story are we building next?

Conclusion

What began as a simple question became a map of patterns shaping everything.

These chapters weren't conclusions, but invitations to see the world with a wider lens.

If beliefs guide us and decisions shape evolution, then every mind is already a part of what comes next.

The patterns will keep shaping us... unless we learn to shape them first.

The world is always sending signals. Evolution begins the moment we choose to notice.

www.ingramcontent.com/pod-product-compliance
Lightning Source LLC
Chambersburg PA
CBHW062203160726
48282CB00027B/978
9789356024397